Book of Numbers For Toddlers & Pre-K Learning

SPEEDY
PUBLISHING

Speedy Publishing LLC
40 E. Main St. #1156
Newark, DE 19711
www.speedypublishing.com

One

TWO

Three

3

Four

Five

5

Six

6

Seven

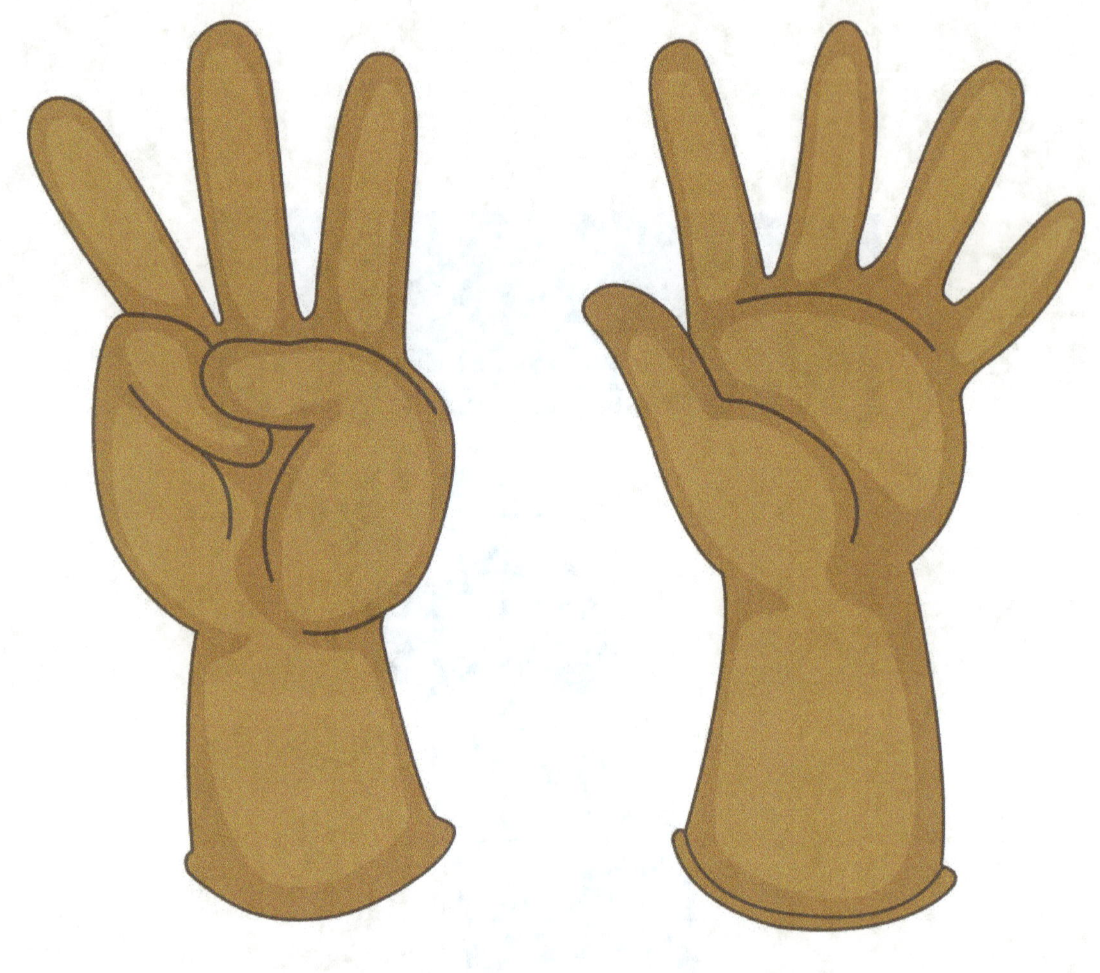

Eight

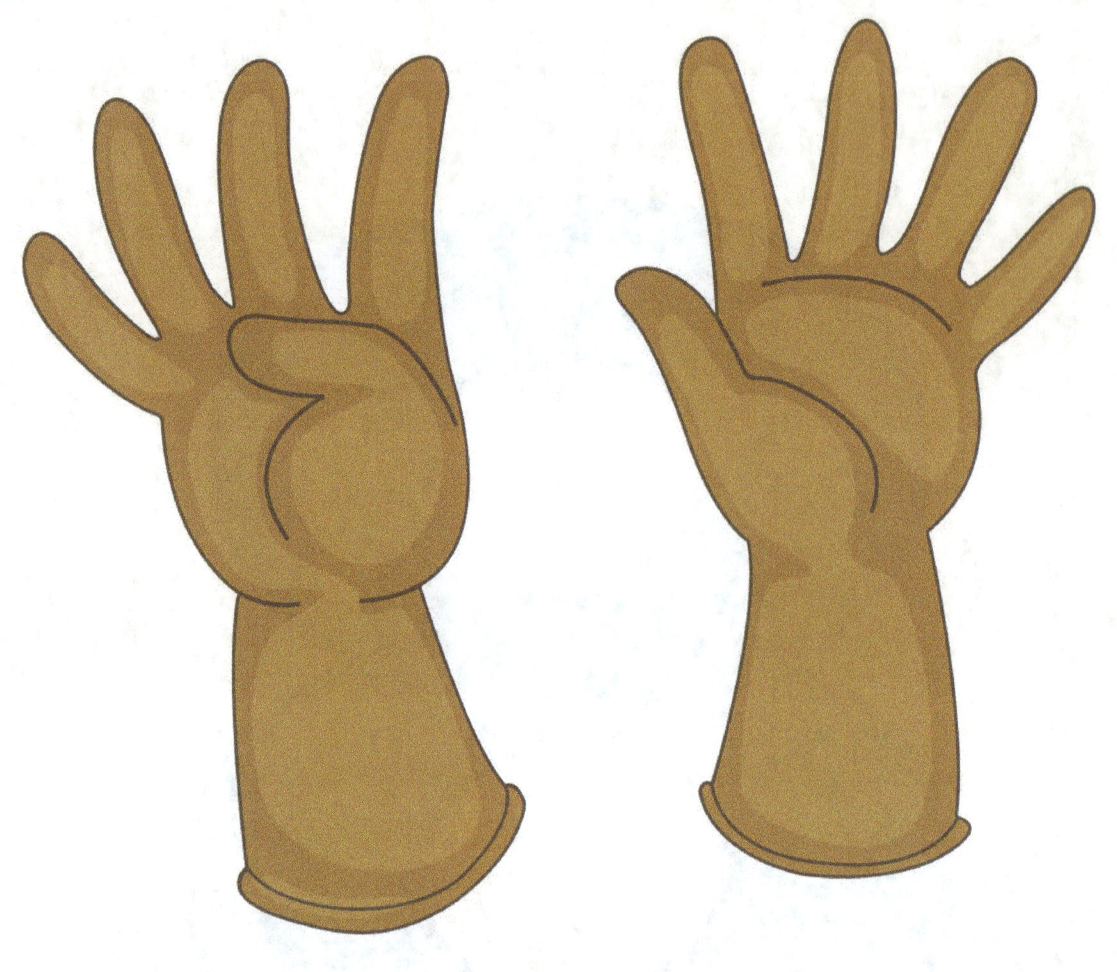

Nine

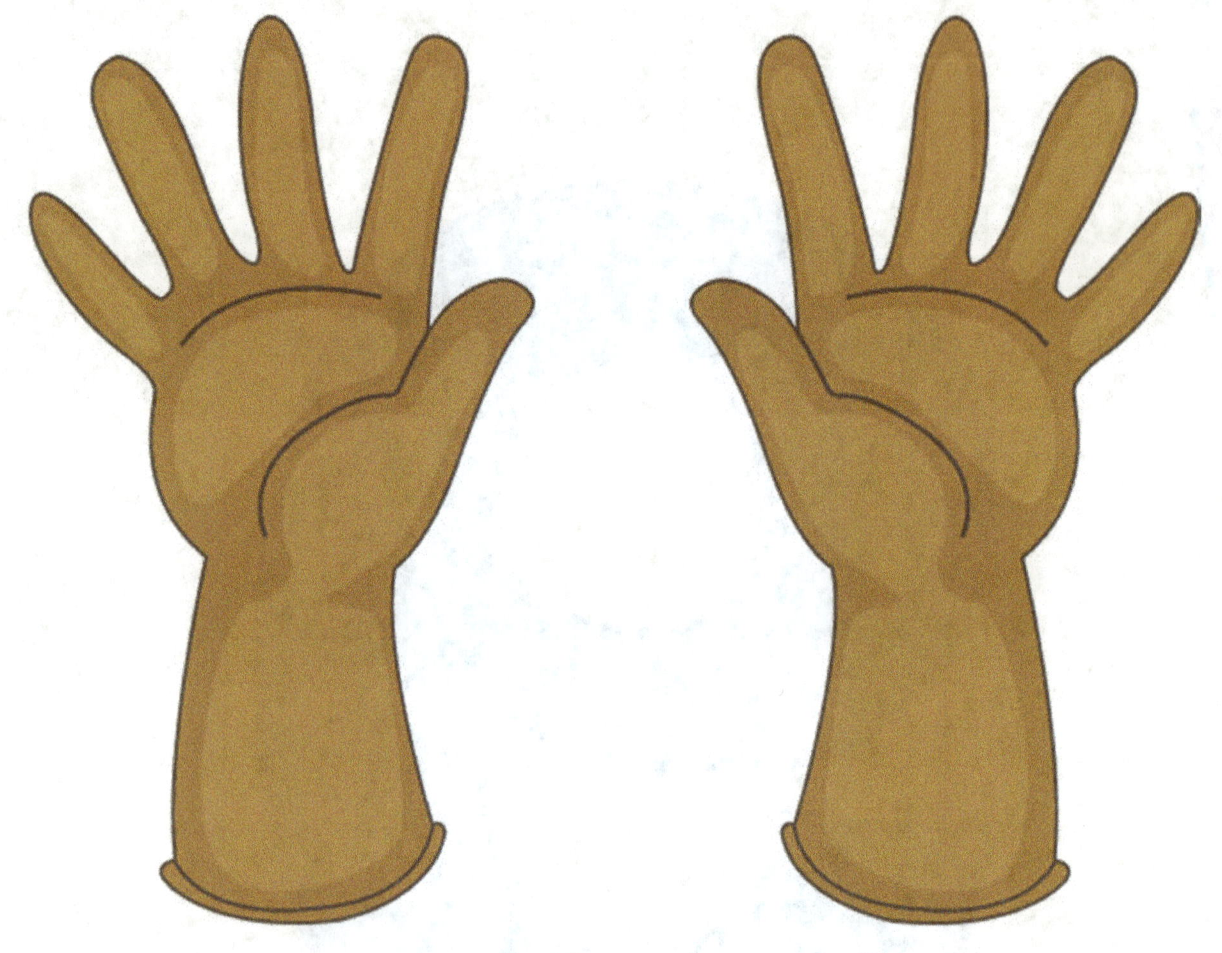

Ten

Let's Count Again!

Color the Numbers!

Practice Writing Numbers!

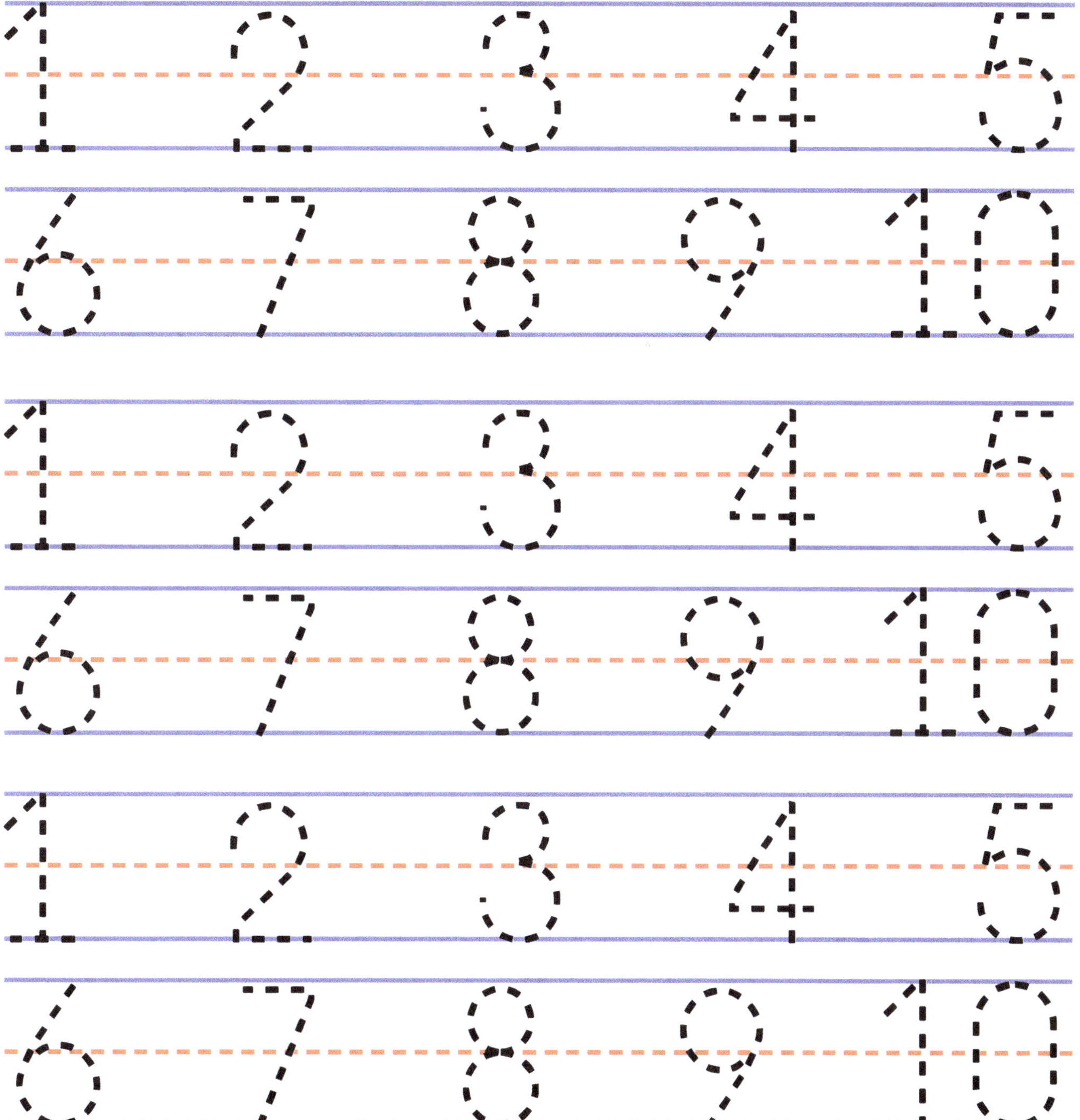

1 2 3 4 5

6 7 8 9 10

1 2 3 4 5

6 7 8 9 10

1 2 3 4 5

6 7 8 9 10

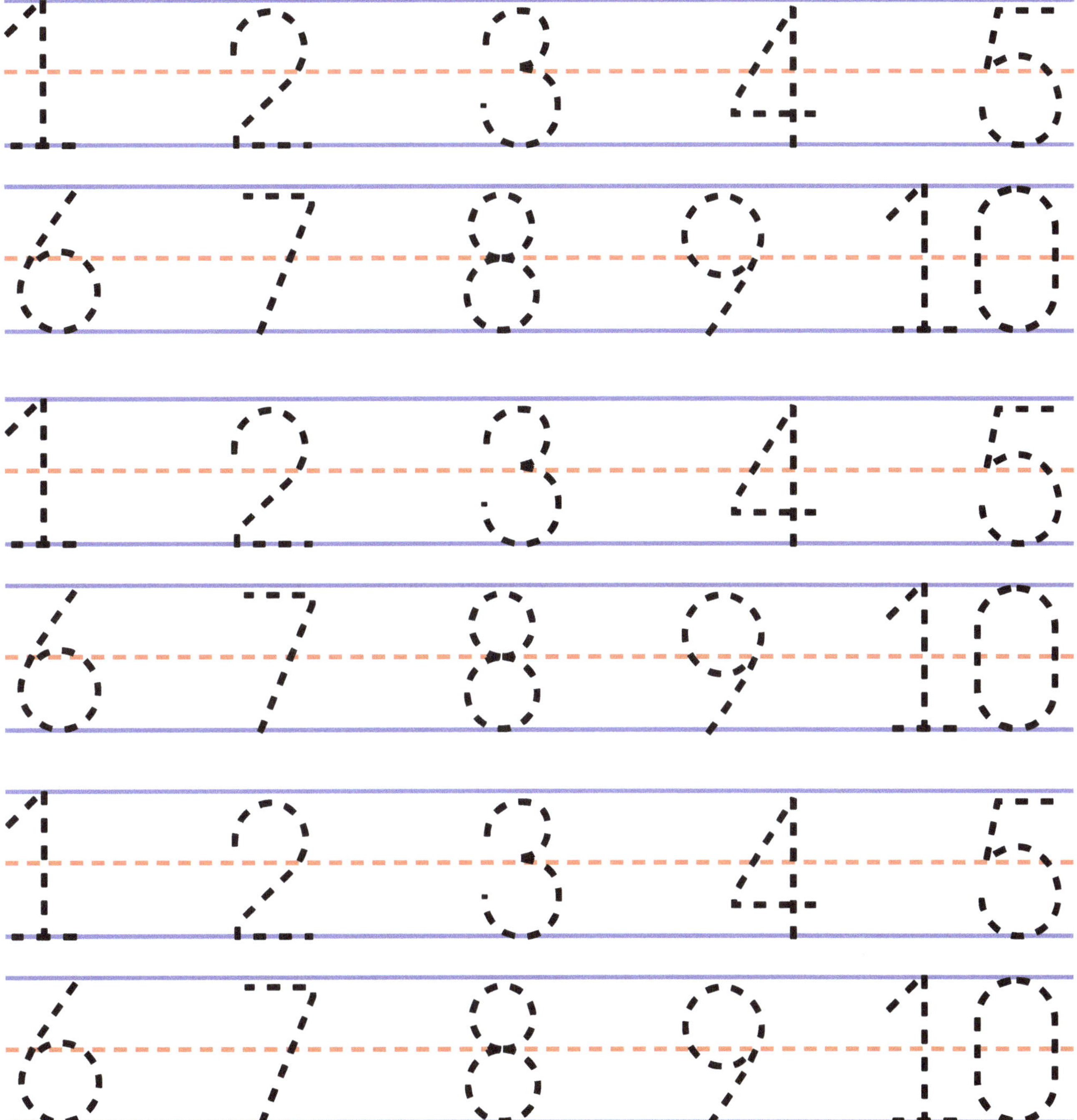